How to Read Fast~

Increase Your Reading Speed
Rate by Practicing Speed Readir.
Can Learn More and Be

By Mitch Jensen

By reading this document, the reader agrees that under no circumstances is the author responsible for any losses, direct or indirect, which are incurred as a result of the use of information contained within this document, including, but not limited to, —errors, omissions, or inaccuracies.

Table of Contents

Thank you for Purchasing this book and I hope that you will find it helpful and useful. If you will want to share your thoughts on this book, you can do so by leaving a review on the Amazon page. It helps me out a lot.

Introduction to Speed Reading

Speed reading is what enables a person to go through the reading material much faster than usual. This is achieved by scanning the parts of the text for keywords or phrases that are relevant in an attempt to extract the meaning without wasting too much time.

As far as comprehending the text itself, most people can comprehend about three quarters of the text they read, but when they attempt to perform the process of speed reading, the comprehension drops from three quarters to below half of the text. This makes it very difficult to understand the material and it can get to the point where it may seem that the person hasn't read anything and can't recall anything that had been read.

A lot of discussions were already had about the topic of speed reading and a lot of money was invested into training courses in an attempt to learn how to go through the information faster by learning how to speed read. Experts are divided when it comes to their stances about speed reading since speed reading may not be well suited for every material out there since they all vary in terms of the complexity of the material which would make the comprehension even tougher. There are also different reasons for reading various materials. Experts think that it is not even worth reading if the comprehension is below 50% since that can't be considered to be an effective learning rate.

Researchers have actually found out that those who went through the material by speed reading through it had a lot more difficulties in recalling details when compared to someone who took their time while going through the material. It is considered that speed readers willingly sacrifice comprehension and absorption in order to gain speed. However, people who are in favor of speed reading tend to name some of the benefits of speed reading such as improvement in IQ and in memory. On the other side, people who aren't as fond of speed reading claim that these claims are bogus and they are willing to go as far as taking legal action against people who hold lectures which show people how to speed read.

Whatever the case may be, it is undeniable that speed reading compromises someone's ability to take in the information he or she is going through. When someone is going through a certain material, they can hear the voice inside their own head and this voice is what helps the person to really get the understanding of the information he or she is taking in. Speed readers are sacrificing this kind of vocalizing inside their heads and that is one of the reasons why comprehension takes a hit during speed reading.

Nevertheless, the tips for those interested in speed reading are as follows:

Before you start with your reading sessions, make sure to preview what you will actually be reading since this will prepare you for the topic and it will allow you to form expectations in terms of what matters and what you should be paying attention to. Just by doing this, you will be a lot more familiar with the essence of the material and reading will be so much easier since you will be able to separate the essential from the nonessential.

Before you actually dive into reading through the material, you want to have some kind of plan. Figure out which paragraphs and which chapters deserve more time than the others based on how challenging to comprehend they may be.

Remember that it is all about the keywords and this realization will make you understand that not all words are equally important and that it is ok to completely ignore some words while still managing to extract the core meaning. In this way you don't need to read the entire sentences, all that you have to do is to read as little as you have to in order to get the meaning. Figure out what the meaning is and then move on. You also want to avoid rereading parts since this will kill your momentum and the flow.

This is something that you have to practice if you want to be good at it and you will get better, the more you practice. Most people read about 240 words per minute, but with speed reading, that number can go up to 700 per minute.

Some people are savants who can manage to get through 10000 words per minute. You read that correctly! What is also amazing is that those same people manage to retain and memorize an impressive amount of information. For those people, even if the comprehension may not be that great, they could easily go through the material again and again until they are certain that they got enough out of it.

It is the fact that speed reading has its upsides and there is a reason why so much money is spent on speed reading courses and seminars year after year. Knowledge is power, and a lot of people want to acquire this skill. The classes about speed reading are even finding their way into the curriculum of certain colleges. For some people, the ideal superpower wouldn't be flying or turning invisible, but rather the ability to extract information from books really fast. Anyone can practice the techniques from the comfort of their own homes and at their own leisure and there are no real barriers to entry.

Chapter 1: Why is Everybody Used to Reading Slowly?

Have you ever asked yourself why is it that some people rush through their books while others take their sweet time to get through a book that may not even be very lengthy? Is it possible that the speed of reading is genetic? Or maybe it is developed and cultivated over time?

To answer some of these questions, it is agreed by the experts that the way in which people read is influenced by how they were taught to read during their childhood. Habits are formed during childhood and they can be either good or bad. However those habits turn out, they will be carried into adulthood. That is why people are different in terms of at what speed they can read through the text.

The aforementioned vocalizing inside the head is what children use to learn how to read. When vocalizing, words are read aloud as they appear in the head. This is how comprehension is built and this is how people take in and understand the information they are faced with.

People in favor of speed reading aren't fond of vocalization and they demean it since they claim that vocalization limits how quickly someone can read and go through the information. There are some exceptions to this and some words that people are so familiar with that they don't even need to say those words inside their head since they can immediately realize what is the meaning behind those words and what is attempted to be conveyed through them. An example of this would be stop signs on the road which tell you to stop even if you just see the red color of the sign.

People who want to increase their reading speed make a conscious effort to reduce the vocalization as they read. Reading quickly is one thing, but it is also necessary to actually comprehend the material and to feel like you got something out of it which isn't always the case with speed reading. That is why there are a lot of people who are against speed reading as a way of going through the material since the comprehension rate drops off for most speed readers from 75% to below 50%. A lot of details may not even be recalled since they weren't even captured during the reading process.

Nevertheless, there are certain bad habits which tend to develop over the lifetime depending on how a person is reading. If a person is not aware of those habits, then those habits may be passed onto the next generation. Some of those bad habits are as follows:

One bad reading habit is reading one word at a time when going through the text. This drastically reduces the reading speed and it also decreases comprehension of the material as a whole, according to the experts. When a reader is focusing on a word for too long, then he may not create the connections within his/her mind about the whole section since he/she is just focusing on words by themselves. In order to comprehend the text, the words have to be read as a group.

Another bad reading habit is going back and rereading the words. This is a habit and it is not something which necessarily has to be done. A lot of slow readers can trace their slow reading speed to this particular habit.

Having a negative outlook towards reading is also something that can be a reason for why someone is a slow reader. These people think that reading is a boring chore and they would choose something more stimulating such as video games or movies in a heartbeat. An education system can, to an extent, be blamed for this since it may seem like the teachers are trying to make reading boring and into something that kids will avoid in the future.

Kids who don't see the value in reading will do what is necessary to just be done with the task of reding so that they could get it out of the way since they see it as a burden. It is necessary to correct this perspective in kids so that they wouldn't continue living while thinking of reading as something that is a necessary evil.

Majority of kids start learning to read when they start with their schooling at the age of 6. It is very important that the children aren't forced to read if they are not ready since this will only frustrate the kids and make them resent reading which is also how problems with reading can form. The fact is that no one can possibly learn to love reading if he or she is forced to read a book which they have no interest in at all and then punished with a bad grade if they don't read it and write a 500-word essay about it. Unfortunately, that is exactly how things are done in schools.

A lot of people who read slowly are not inherently slow readers, it is all due to some bad habits which they may not even be aware of and which act as a massive invisible obstacle. There is hope, however, and if someone is aware of these bad reading habits in themselves, then action can be taken and slow readers can start increasing their reading speed bit by bit.

Chapter 2: Who is Speed Reading for?

People start to turn letters, symbols and sounds into sentences which convey meaning as early as during their childhood. This is how the skill of reading is developed and it should be nurtured through life in order for comprehension and speed to keep improving.

The skill of reading is what makes it possible for people to understand what they read and to gain comprehension. This is how knowledge is acquired and that knowledge can be applied in everyday life to achieve what a person wants to achieve.

Information is very important in today's world and it is necessary to know how to read well in order to get ahead. People who can go through the information quicker and comprehend it better, tend to be better off financially instead of someone who reads and comprehends at the average rate. This is the reason why speed reading came to fruition as a technique which makes it possible for the people to read a lot more words per minute.

There is a lot of marketing about the greatness of speed reading, but it is necessary to take a step back and ask yourself is there validity to this or is it all just hype. In order to determine this, it is necessary to be familiar with the data:

An average reader reads around 240 words per minute. This reading speed usually applies to fiction books and simple non-technical books. This reading speed of an average reader is also the one which makes comprehension quite possible.

There is no shortage of ads which promise you that the course they are advertising can get you to the point of being able to read 10000 words per minute just like a savant, without all the drawbacks of being a savant. However, nothing is usually mentioned about the comprehension, and ultimately it really may not matter that much if you can rush through the material if you can hardly remember what you had read and the details about it.

Triple or quadruple reading speed can be achieved, but you might want to think about if the possible reduction in comprehension is worth it. Then again, since you are reading fast, you can always go through the material again. It is very helpful to be aware of which kinds of people in which situations can really benefit from the skill of speed reading.

Students, both in high school and college, have a lot of text through which they have to get through in order to complete their education. If the comprehension can be maintained, then the skill of speed reading can be very handy for them since they still have to understand what they read in order to pass the exams and that is why they shouldn't be neglecting comprehension. Photographic memory is one tool of speed reading which can be handy for students who can master it.

Speed reading can be useful to many people who are in a business, whether as a business owner or as an employee. Most positions will be faced with a lot of documentation and memos that simply have to be handled every single day. It is essential to be able to go through the information in order to be with the times and to know what is happening in the industry. Speed reading can be very helpful for these people since it can allow them to quickly go through the information so that they could go back to performing key business activities.

Next group of people who could improve their situation with speed reading are people with medical disabilities. Around 15% of children fall into this group. People in this group read way slower than they should. If people in this group took to the time to practice the principles of speed reading, they could improve their situation drastically.

People who suffer from the attention-deficit disorder, or ADD for short, can benefit from speed reading since they are forced to read so quickly and to go through the words so quickly that they simply don't get the opportunity to get bored. These people are more likely to wander since they have a shorter attention span and that is why speed reading can be used to focus them.

Ultimately, it is necessary to know when it is appropriate and necessary to apply the skill of speed reading. For example, someone who wants to sit on a beach and a go through a book will have a better time with only one book instead of carrying around 10 books which would be skimmed through. In this situation, rushing through the books would suck out the pleasure and the enjoyment out of the activity.

At the end of the day, you should be aware of why you are attempting to learn speed reading and what you are trying to get out of it. You should also have an understanding of what role does reading have in your life.

Chapter 3: Is Speed Reading in the Genes or is it Something That Can Be Acquired?

When most people learn to read, they focus on one letter at a time. As people get older, they learn to read groups of words and phrases. Speed reading is learned in a similar way.

Most people are convinced that speed reading is genetic and that it is something a person is born with, but the fact is that it is a skill which can be gained through practice and repetition. The goal should be to consume larger quantities of information each time you go through a certain text. You should also aim to increase the speed at which you can process the information.

As mentioned, the average reading speed is around 240 words per minute, while top speed readers can manage to go through 10000 words per minute which is the same as getting through 70 pages in one minute. Still, if you want to do well in education or in business, you have to know how to read fast while still keeping your comprehension high.

Before you start reading anything, you should be aware of the context and of what you are looking for so that you know how to recognize the things you are attempting to discover. After you know what you are looking for, you should go through the chunks of information while extracting the valuable bits which are related to what you are looking for and which are important.

If someone is a good reader, that person can read more words per chunk of information and this allows for that reader to maintain a consistent and fluid pace of reading. Conversely, a less capable reader will need more time just to read fewer words. This person will likely skip words and this will make it harder to get into the flow of reading.

Another thing which is necessary to focus on is the movement of the eyes since reading will be a lot harder for someone who doesn't move their eyes with some kind of regularity. In order to speed read well, it is necessary to know how to focus the eyes so that more information could be extracted. The more information the reader can extract per chunk of information, the faster he or she will be able to read.

The information is grouped into chunks and speed reading is largely about increasing sizes of chunks someone can read through. Speed readers can go through the text quickly because they read chunk by chunk instead of reading word by word. As mentioned, the reading can be done faster if the chunks which a reader can comprehend are larger and filled with more words.

It is also necessary that a reader learns to get through the chunk of information faster and this can be improved over time through practice and patience and not giving up.

It is necessary to stop rereading since that hugely slows down the pace at which text can be read. As the reading speed gets slower and slower, the more a person goes back to read through the text.

There is no way to get good at speed reading without practice and doing so a lot. Each person is different, and it is necessary to try out and to experiment with different reading tricks in order to learn how to really read faster. One trick is using a certain waypoint such as a ruler which is moved down the page at your own speed so that you could more easily focus on where you are at with your reading. Try to move a ruler without stopping or hesitation so that you clear a certain page in one single sweep. This can be a bit awkward at first, but you will get better with practice and you will start moving the ruler faster as you start reading faster.

In order to measure your progress, you should be attempting to read through chunks faster and you will know that you are getting better if you manage to read through a chunk of similar size faster.

As it was mentioned many times, speed reading is a skill and skills are developed by deliberately practicing them over time. You won't become a speed reader in a week. You may not be able to read 70 pages per minute like some people, but managing to increase your reading speed even a little can benefit you a lot and can make you more effective.

Chapter 4: Test Your Reading Speed!

Do you think that you can read through an entire novel at once? Can you read the whole newspaper from front to back? Do you think that your reading speed is of a tortoise or of a hare? You can always find out how fast you are able to read.

One quick and easy way of finding out how fast you can read is to look up a reading test online. There are plenty of websites which will allow you to test your reading speed free of charge. This works by measuring the time in which you can read through the text which is shown to you. You can start and stop the timer at your convenience.

The point of this test is to read the text at your normal speed since you want to get a precise measurement here. One interesting fact is that most people read text on screens slower than they would read that same text in a book.

When you finish reading the text, you can stop the timer to see what your reading speed is like. You want to do some calculations in order to determine how many words you read per minute since you already know that most people can read around 240 words per minute. Based on the result, you can determine what your reading speed is like when compared to average.

There are also websites where you can take a test which will measure your memory and comprehension. These kinds of tests start similarly with a participant reading through the text which is presented. After you are done with reading, you are posed with questions relating to the text you just went through. You have to answer these questions based on what you had read since you aren't allowed to read the text again in hope of finding an answer. The more answers you get right, the higher your score is.

When you speed read through a text, you are going through it faster, but your comprehension of that text suffers as a result. Decreased ability to absorb the information and to be able to recall more details is the price that has to be paid in order to speed read. That is why the text for the purposes of memory and comprehension measurement has to be read at a normal pace.

Going through the text quickly is nice, but what may be more important is actually understanding and retaining what you had read. According to the experts, you should only be worried if your level of comprehension dips below 50%.

When someone is speed reading, that person is reading way faster than what is considered to be an average reading speed. This is done by skimming through the text in question instead of reading one word at a time. This way, it is attempted to figure out the essence of the text.

This is all well and god, but the comprehension of the reader takes a dive as a consequence. Learning new things isn't easy, but it gets even harder when it is done like this.

When attempting to figure out someone's reading speed, there are factors that should be taken into consideration. It is helpful to know in which way was a person taught how to read. It is necessary to also know how old was a person when that person was introduced to reading. It also helps if it is clear how well a person can focus their attention over an extended period on a task such as reading. Not all reading material is the same, and it helps knowing what kind of material is being read by a person. Finally, it is also necessary to be aware of the amount of vocalizing that is occurring while the person is doing the reading.

When someone is vocalizing a word, they are saying the word aloud that is in their head at the moment. Speed reading experts look down upon vocalizing aloud since they believe that the reading speed is negatively impacted by doing that. Even though vocalizing may slow down the speed of reading, there are people who say that vocalization actually enhances learning. Proponents of vocalization claim that the information is absorbed more effectively this way. You can still understand the material without the vocalization, but not to the same extent.

A lot of hard earned money was spent on books and courses that teach speed reading, but many experts still claim that there isn't much use in speed reading without proper comprehension. This is where being aware of how fast you can read helps, since you can know whether you need to work on your base reading speed or not. Anyone can benefit from taking these tests of reading speed.

Chapter 5: How to Measure Your Reading Skill

There is another way which you can use in order to see how good you are at reading. Before you try that, it is necessary to be aware of the role of reading in our history. Ever since the alphabet existed, reading has been an essential part of human life. People read each and every that, and that will not change. No one can get through a day without having to read something. Reading is essential, but the fact is that not every person can read at the same speed and the same level of efficiency. The people who tend to read the fastest and most efficiently are in the minority and they can go through a lot more material than the average reader.

There are reasons for the fact that minority of the people tend to have the most skill when it comes to reading. The fact is that not every person places the same attention and importance to their reading speed. Even some people that aren't exactly happy with their reading speed believe that they can't do much to improve their situation. Some people also think that the skill of reading faster isn't necessarily something that is worth the improvement. Most people think that learning to type faster will be more beneficial than learning how to read faster.

The truth is that reading stems from the habits that a person acquired ever since that person could read. These aren't the things that can be changed so easily and it takes time to change habits since people are creatures of habit and they don't always like change.

One such habit is the vocalization which limits the speed at which the text which is read can be processed and comprehended. Movement of the eyes and general focus also place a limit on what someone can see since rereading and going back to read certain parts of the text more than once increases the amount of time that is spent reading. Not being able to concentrate adequately and not having wide enough vocabulary also decreases reading speed since understanding the text gets more difficult as a result.

The issue could actually lie in not having accurate information about reading itself and the reading habits. This understanding can be gained by taking the aforementioned test of reading speed as well as the test which would measure the comprehension of the text which is being read.

There is an additional method of testing the reading speed. In order to start with this method, it is necessary to choose two quality reading materials. Each reading material doesn't have to be longer than a page. The complexity of the material should be just right, it shouldn't be too difficult or too easy to understand. For each reading material, you want to start off by counting how many words there are per a line of text and then counting how many lines of text there are per page. Write these results down.

Next, you want to have another person who will read both the texts. After they have finished reading, they should come up with a couple of questions which can all be answered by someone who has read the texts in question.

The next step is to read the first page while not having enough time to finish reading that page at your usual reading speed. While reading, you want to be paying attention to the things that make reading harder for you and which slow it down. When you are done reading, you want to immediately write down all the difficulties you may have come across.

For the next step, you need a timer. Once you have a timer, measure the time it takes you to read the second page entirely and write down the time required when you are done reading. When you have written down your time, then it is time to answer the questions that were compiled by the other person.

The next step is to calculate your reading speed and you do this by multiplying the values from the first step, which are the number of words per line of text as well as the number of lines of text per page. The result of this multiplication has to be divided by the amount of time in minutes which is needed to finish reading the text. The number you get is your reading speed.

You also want to measure your comprehension and you can do so by dividing the number of answers you got right by the total number of questions that were asked by another participant. The result of this division should be multiplied by 100 in order to get the percentage value of the comprehension.

The final step of this test is the evaluation. As mentioned, average reading speed is about 240 words per minute while the more efficient readers can manage to get through 1000 words per minute while still maintaining a good rate of comprehension.

The same measurement of reading speed can be done by visiting one of the websites and taking the reading speed test, although the results that are obtained this way tend to differ since different methods are utilized and you will generally get the most accurate assessment by going through the method which was just described.

You should also remember that you can generally read quicker when reading of paper instead of reading something that is written on the screen. When you measure your reading speed and you are aware of it, you are a step closer to becoming a more efficient reader. When you know yourself and you understand how you tend to read, you are more able to figure out the best course of action for increasing your reading speed.

Chapter 6: How to Test Your Ability to Retain the Information

While testing your reading speed is well and good, you still don't want to forget about the comprehension since there isn't much point in reading something that you can't even remember when you are done with reading. You want to focus on both being able to go through a certain material quickly while also extracting the important information and knowledge. This is a skill that can be very useful to any individual, both in personal and in professional life.

You want to know where you stand when compared to the average reading speed which is about 240 words per minute. If your reading speed is below this average speed, you should first figure out the reasons behind this. Some mistakes you may be making while reading are being laser-focused on one point with your eyes while you are reading, reading the text in your mind and rereading certain parts of the text such as phrases or paragraphs which usually happens when your concentration takes a hit.

It is really helpful if you are aware of these habits that can slow down your reading speed. Additionally, there are things you can start doing immediately in order to read faster.

In order to read faster, you should know beforehand what you are hoping to get out of the material you are reading. For example, a student who is preparing for an exam should focus on the things that are most likely to come up as questions. An employee who does a job where he/she has to work with data inevitably has to go through numerous reports. For those people, it is important to know how to distinguish between the details and the important stuff so that the focus could be placed on what is important. Reports can be read faster by focusing on the important stuff while skimming through details. By being aware of what is attempted to be found out when reading through the material, the reading speed can be improved significantly.

Another thing you can do in order to increase your reading speed is to try to really take in more words as you are going through the reading material. If you want to increase your reading speed, then you have to practice. You want to proceed with the exercise at your own pace. The goal is to take things one step at a time and to get better at grouping words into chunks. You need to be practicing if you want to be able to group words into larger and larger chunks and you will improve at this as long as you practice and are consistent with your practice.

It is important to remember to do this at your own pace without external pressure since you don't want to sacrifice the rate of retention. When you read through a document, you want to test yourself by thinking about what you remember from the material you just read. You should try to make a summary of what you have read in your mind.

One more way to increase your reading speed is to increase your focus. By increasing your focus, you will prevent your attention from going astray unconsciously, because when this happens you will inevitably have to go back to reading again through the words you should have already read through. You can avoid this by using a pointer such as a finger or a pencil while you are going along with your reading. If you are reading on a computer screen, then you can use a mouse pointer which you will move as you are moving along with the reading. It is easier to achieve a sense of flow in reading when your eyes have something which they should clearly follow. The goal is to always move forward with your reading since going back and rereading what you should only be reading once is a waste of your time. Keep doing this, and your reading speed is bound to increase.

If you want to improve the speed of your reading, there are also seminars and courses which you can attend with that purpose in mind. Whether you should take a course or not, depends on how well you did on the test that measures your reading speed and your retention. If you consider that your reading speed is not up to par, and you want to get it increased as quickly as possible, then paying for one of the courses or seminars may be a worthwhile expense.

Chapter 7: The Importance of Tracking Your Progress

It is a very good idea to have a reading habit since more and more people have started turning to the screen for education ever since the advent of the television. Introduction of more options for entertainment has discouraged a lot of people from reading. Reading is still unmatched when it comes to acquiring knowledge.

Video and audio format is pretty prevalent in all walks of life, but that doesn't change the role which reading has in everyday life. Everyone spends an hour or so a day reading whether they are aware of it or not. This reading can range from newspapers to bills and various documents that have to be read as part of someone's work.

Even though most people have a lot of opportunities to read via books, news articles and various documents, the average reading speed rarely deviates from the reading speed of 240 words per minute. The average comprehension rate is between 50 and 60 percent for most people.

The reason for the reading speed stopping at this average speed may lie in the aforementioned reading habits that slow down reading such as reading the words in the mind or aloud. This kind of vocalization delays the reading speed since the individual tends to wait until the word is heard entirely before continuing with the reading. It's a fact that reading would be much faster without this form of delaying. Another common issue could lie in being fixated on a certain word before moving on with the reading material.

Speed reading can also be halted by rereading the text and going back. Rereading a word or a chunk of words is not the way to go. Another common issue could lie in being fixated on a certain word before moving on with the reading material. This could be caused by a tendency to get fixated on a word for too long or it can be caused by a lack of concentration.

In order to be proficient at a skill of reading, it is necessary for the mind and the eyes to work well together. Just like any other skill, there are several ways to improve the skill of reading. In order to get better at the skill of reading, you have to set clear goals. When you set goals, you are focusing on what you want to accomplish based on where you are at the moment. You can figure out where you are by determining your reading speed by applying one of the methods that were already mentioned, such as online reading tests.

If you want to learn how to read faster, you should first be aware of why you reading something. If someone is reading something as a part of leisure activity, then it is not necessary to apply pressure to that situation, while articles are usually read faster.

On the other hand, serious and technical books aren't as easy to read and it is necessary to first become somewhat familiar with the reading material before truly diving into reading. You can do this by checking out summaries of a book or a synopsis that may be located at the end of the book or at the end of each chapter. The comprehension can also be improved by checking out reviews of the book and the information about the author of the book.

This may seem like a lot of work and you may ask yourself whether all that prep work is worth it. There are good reasons for learning how to read faster and they can be used as motivation. Speed reading can actually make reading itself more fun. When you know how to read fast, then you can get to the essence of what the author is trying to say that much quicker. If you can read faster, you can learn new things much faster. People who are thirsty for knowledge will find a lot of motivation in this reason. Speed reading can acquire you to gain new perspectives in less time.

Students who can speed read can achieve better grades. Students are faced with a lot of material they have to read through in order to stay on top of their papers and assignments. Speed reading can make sure that these assignments get done faster and the sooner those assignments get done, the better. Students can have even more time to enjoy their student experience this way.

When someone knows how to speed read, then that person can do better in their career. Any knowledge worker has a lot of documents and data he/she has to go through and the one who can deal with all that stuff the fastest will be the one who gets things done faster. A person who can speed read can choose between producing more results and having more free time for leisure and self-improvement.

When someone can read faster, then there is more time for other activities since all the necessary evil such as assignments and reports are taken care of quicker. This frees up a lot of time for other things and hobbies you may want to invest your time in and pursue.

Interestingly enough, someone who can read fast can also increase their ability in other areas of life. Someone who can read fast and who can go through certain material faster can grasp novel ideas faster and more effectively.

Someone who is able to read faster will have more self-confidence and self-esteem. Self-confidence stems from the knowledge that goals that are set can be accomplished. It does make a person feel better when they can do something quickly which others struggle with. Being ahead of the curve is what strengthens self esteem.

Comprehension can be actually improved by speed reading. Even though reading faster can decrease understanding, knowing how to chunk words and to read them like that can only be achieved by someone who understands the meaning of the material.

Speed reading allows a person to diversify their knowledge. Someone who can read fast can go through the information in less time. This essentially means that a person can go through a lot of information in a certain period of time. This is how more layers are added to someone's knowledge. It can actually be said that reading faster can extend someone's life, especially when a person can read through a book in 4 hours which would otherwise require 10 hours of reading at a regular pace.

Finally, speed reading can lead to improvement in someone's financial situation. Someone who can read faster can get through more books faster. This means that a person who can read fast has the ability to read more on the topic of money and business.

Chapter 8: What You Should Know About Speed Reading Classes

If someone is a less efficient reader, then there is no need to worry since there is a way to improve. Reading is a skill and skills can be improved by practice and repetition as long as the right tools and techniques are utilized.

Did you ever read a book without understanding what it is about afterward? Are you reading the text word by word while also saying the words aloud? Is your reading speed below the average of 240 words per minute? People who answer positively to most of those question tend to be less efficient readers. These people tend to read parts of the text several times and they have a chance of getting stuck shortly on a certain part of the text.

The good thing is that people who aren't happy with their reading speed have more motivation to improve their situation and they will be more inclined to buy books about speed reading or to invest in courses. Anyone, regardless of their age, can attend speed reading classes since those classes are available to everyone. The results from these classes will actually have the most impact on children who are in primary school, even though adults can still benefit from speed reading classes.

If the right tools and methods are used when teaching children how to speed read, the results can be noticed as soon as one month has been spent in a speed reading class. It is necessary to remember that everyone is different and that not everyone learns at the same speed.

What is the reason for attending speed reading classes? There are a lot of situations in which knowing how to read fast can be a useful skill to have. When you know how to read fast, you can save a lot of time while also going through a lot of quality information. If someone knows how to read fast, they have valuable tools and tricks they can use to read faster, along with improved memory and productivity.

What should you know before you decide to join a speed reading course? Obviously, you should have the financial resources in order to purchase a course, but aside from that, you should have good enough comprehension and vocabulary. You should also be good at reading at a basic level as well since speed reading classes are about improving the reading speed instead of teaching the reading from the ground up. The age isn't something you should be concerned with since anyone who can read is eligible for a reading course.

Speed reading courses focus on teaching participants some speed reading techniques such as skimming through the text and scanning the words in the text in order to distinguish the essence from the details. The exercises in speed reading courses consist of reading for a certain period of time and then having to answer questions which serve as a test of information retention and memory.

Speed reading is something that can't be learned overnight and it is necessary to put in the work and to take learning this skill seriously. It is normal for people who start with speed reading classes to not get much out of them at first, but when proper techniques and tools are finally learned and internalized and can be used naturally without any external pressure, then it can be said that students have learned to speed read properly. The goal is to get the students to able to use their speed reading skill in any situation which requires that something is read quickly.

However, speed reading courses are not just about tips and tricks. These courses also focus on teaching students how to read a nonfiction book while maintaining a good understanding and taking good notes. Fiction books aren't ignored either and it
is taught how to dissect the story so that more can be gained from the reading itself.

The speed reading courses usually start off with participants measuring how efficient they currently are at reading and that is done by multiplying the words that are read per minute with the rate of comprehension. Students are also made aware of the possible bad reading habits which were a part of their reading unconsciously. These bad reading habits are the usual suspects such as reading words in your mind and aloud while reading, reading with bad lighting, reading with bad posture etc. The end goal of these speed reading classes is to minimize these bad reading habits while improving speed reading proficiency by getting better at scanning keywords and chunking text into groups.

Chapter 9: Reading and the Eyes

People who work in offices tend to spend a lot of time looking at the screen as a part of their duties. They could be doing many things on the computer, such as doing some research or surfing the web. People even eat their lunch in front of the screen.

When people come home from work, they are likely to go back to the screen again to do one of many things such as watching movies, playing video games or reading ebooks. It is not surprising to experience tears and blurry vision at the end of the day. If this describes you, then you need to take care of your eyes seriously and you should start doing it as soon as possible.

You have heard that eyes are the windows to your soul. Eyes are also a vital organ which enables you to read and to make sense of all the data you are receiving. The eyes are like a camera, the images you see go through the lens and the cornea and are focused on the retina. The retina is where the light is processed and sent to the brain.

Do you want to know how your eyes work during the reading? When you are reading, regardless if it is from a paper or a screen, your eyes tend to focus and to follow the words as you read them. Reading can actually put a lot of pressure on your eyes. It doesn't get much better if reading is done via a screen. There are many things that can lead to some eye problems if they are performed longer than it is healthy, such as reading, looking at a screen too much, playing video games etc.

These activities are perfectly fine, I am a video gamer myself, but you have to learn how to take care of your eyes when they get tired. This may be the most important chapter in the book, so make sure to pay attention.

You can rest your eyes by looking into the distance, or by taking a walk and letting your eyes relax. You can also blink consciously since blinking is to the eyes what the wiper is to the windshield of a car.

There are issued that can be caused by reading and it is important to be aware of those since they are recognized by medical experts. You should check if you may be experiencing some of the issues already. Being nearsighted is a quite common eye issue and for people who have this, objects that are far away tend to be blurry. On the other end, people who are farsighted see the objects that are close to them as blurry.

Astigmatism is a combination of these two issues and it consists of seeing both the distant and near objects as blurry. Thankfully, it is quite easy to deal with this issue by putting on prescribed glasses or contact lenses. Laser treatment such as LASIK is also an option.

Taking care of the eyes is important for obvious reasons, but eye issue can also negatively impact reading and learning. Some people may be mistakenly considered to not be as smart just because they may not have the same ability to properly see the information. These people may not be dumb at all, they are just experiencing some problems with their vision which can be remedied via a therapy.

Some parents may be convinced that their kids are slow learners while the issue may be of the visual kind. These parents should consult with an optometrist in order to see what is truly going on.

If you suspect that you yourself or someone you know has an issue with learning through reading, there are certain signs you should pay attention to. Maybe someone is reading a word wrong because they are substituting the letters mistakenly, maybe they are complaining that they get tired from reading, maybe they skip lines during reading, maybe they are going back and rereading the text. When these signs are notices, an optometrist should be consulted in order to be certain whether an issue exists or not.

Vision is actually also a skill, just like speed reading and it can be improved. Having good eyesight and good eye health is essential to be successful with speed reading. Through good vision, you are able to make sense of what is around you. It is important to be aware of the movement of your eyes since this has an impact on how you will process the information. For example, blinking faster can be seen as a sign of nervousness.

We were all probably scolded by parents for reading in a badly lit environment. They actually may be onto something there since reading in an environment that isn't illuminated enough cause your pupils to expand and that leads to more blur which actually makes a person temporarily nearsighted.

If you want to be certain that your eyes are alright so that you continue reading and doing what you like without an issue, you should have your eyes checked out by a professional every now and then.

Chapter 10: How Important are Your Hands When Reading?

Hands have an effect on reading comprehension. A mind becomes more active when the hands are involved. The readers are already familiar at this point with the fact that reading from a screen and from a paper is not the same thing.

It is a fact that people have a harder time understanding what is written on a screen than understanding something that is written on paper. Interestingly, the same information will be perceived as being less convincing if it is read from a screen as opposed to something that is read of a paper such as stories and articles.

The first stimuli that were developed in the upper part of the human body are gestures. Toddlers learn about the world and about the people through gestures and the things they see first once they are aware. Toddlers will learn from anything that piques their curiosity. Once a toddler's mind is stimulated by something, they continue their learning further through the use of hands. They touch and feel the things which got their attention and that is how they acquire their understanding of the world.

Over time, the brain gets acclimated to this and that is how their brain develops. That is how toddlers learn to coordinate the movement of their hands. It is completely natural for humans to learn to read with the help of their hands and it has been that way for millions of years. Every following generation of ancient humans learned by examining the stone carvings of their predecessors. The eyes and hands had to be working together in order to read those images successfully. The touching had to be done along with seeing in order to figure out the whole meaning that can't be gained from just looking at the set of symbols. Those images served as a representation of their thoughts and emotion at the time of carving.

This kind of comprehension was passed down from generation to generation over the course of time and a lot of it rubbed off on us today. The only major change is in how the reading itself was influenced by the development of the technology. Even something as subtle as physically flipping a page of the book impacts learning in a way that makes it easier for new concepts to be grasped. Comprehension simply happens when fingers glide along with the words on a paper. This is because remembering the location of the finger and the hand during the time of reading enhances learning.

If someone happened to be using a hand as a guiding tool during the reading, they are a lot more likely to recall the information in question. Nothing drastic has to occur during the reading process, all that is required is that the reading material is held in the hand or for a person to be located in a place where reading took place in order for the information in question to be recalled. The hands and the location are used as a cue.

Hands certainly have a role in the process of reading. Paper isn't the only medium through which reading can happen. Hand gestures and similar signs can be used to accomplish a goal of communicating something. Some people's job is dependent on the effective utilization of hand gestures, traffic coordinator being one example of that.

People prefer to hold a document of some kind instead of reading the information of the same kind from a screen or a poster on a wall. This ensures that the rate of retention remains high while the chance of making mistakes goes way down.

When reading is done with the aid of the hands, concepts can be comprehended much easier. When some important piece of information is came across during the reading process, hands serve a very useful function of serving as a medium through which emotions can be expressed. An example of this would be pointing with a finger at the words which are deemed important according to certain criteria, and in this way, the information acquisition is enhanced by the reaction.

When a person actually has the opportunity to read something while holding a book, that is how they get a better understanding of what is attempted to be conveyed by a book. This can also act as the process of getting to know the author of the book personally. The same feeling simply can't be captured when the same sort of content is read from a screen. It is so much more rewarding to read a piece of information that is bound to a book or a paper since the hands can be used to enhance the learning in order to really drill the concepts into the brain.

Chapter 11: Is There a Difference Between Reading Fiction and Nonfiction?

It is not recommended to take reading for granted as it has an important function in the history of humans. Humans are only known species which conveys messages and meaning through the utilization of symbols. It is quite easy to understand why people are so motivated to improve their communication more than anything else.

Communication is very important for any human since humans are social species and the overall health and wellbeing will depend largely upon the successful conduct with others. There are many ways to achieve communication, some of those ways are through voice, images or symbols which are used to create associations with things which are attempted to be communicated.

When someone reads, he or she is attempting to retrieve and to understand the information by using appropriate symbols which should indicate what is attempted to be conveyed. Reading is great because it gives us the opportunity to learn from the experiences and perspectives of someone else. Reading is pretty entertaining as well and it can be a good form of escapism from the daily reality and daily worries and there is a peaceful sense of calmness when doing so.

Most books which exist can be grouped in one of two categories. Books can either be fiction or nonfiction. Fiction books are a result of someone's imagination and creativity from which fictional situations and stories are created. There can be a lot of realism in fiction if a person who writes it decides to sprinkle in their own experiences from life. Fiction lives and dies on the author's ability to tell a compelling story. People love stories.

Most people view fiction as something that is done with the goal of entertainment. There is a reason for this, and that is because fiction tends to appeal to emotions due to the way it is written. Fiction literature can make a person forget about the day to day stuff, they can make a person look at life from a different angle and they can also spark many emotions such as laughter, crying and empathy even though the things that are written about aren't even real. Some fiction genres and examples are myths, comics, novels, fairy tales, and so on.

The next main category of books in nonfiction and this includes books in which an author focuses on a certain topic from the real world. Nonfiction books are representations of facts. One possible issue with works of nonfiction lies in the fact that the material may not be understood by everyone since such works are generally targeted at a specific audience with specific issues which are attempted to be addressed with a nonfiction book.

There are a lot of possibilities with nonfiction and some examples of nonfiction literature are biographies, essays, documentaries, journals, encyclopedias, manuals, scientific papers, dictionaries, guides, magazines, newspaper, technical how-to books, textbooks, low content and no content books such as diaries, articles, business information such as accounting ledgers and so on.

Works of fiction mostly focus on getting the reader's imagination to work. If a writer of fiction is a good one, then the reader is able to suspend belief in order to be entertained. On the other hand, the nonfiction authors primarily focus on conveying factual information, but they will throw in some entertainment if it makes sense since no one likes to read something that is too dry and that feels like just an information dump.

No matter which category of books you look at, all of them require creativity and imagination in order to convey the facts to the readers in a compelling way. When reading a good work of fiction, it can be easy to achieve a flow state in which there are no worries anymore. A good work of fiction can take a reader beyond their senses and into a whole new world.

Regardless of what kind of book is being read, readers want to get their entertainment. Good fiction writers know how to make things interesting. When reading works of fiction, there is an underlying theme that ties everything together. The usual elements of a story are a protagonist, the antagonist and the plot of some kind. It is also necessary to know how to set a scene so that a book would have a certain flavor to itself. The story itself should be well paced and, ideally, all should be leading to a climax or a resolution of some sort.

There are numerous genres of fiction such as romance, science fiction, historical fiction, fantasy, western, mythical, cyberpunk and so on.

The works of nonfiction aren't as flexible, but over time, nonfiction writers made an effort to make the works of nonfiction more entertaining for the readers while not neglecting to keep the readers informed about the main point of the book. Still, it won't be possible for each and every nonfiction title to be entertaining to read. Accounting books would be a good example of such books.

Chapter12: Speed Reading and Vocalization

You are probably aware of the fact that you are receiving more and more daily information as the time goes on. Whenever a certain article is written, every person who reads that article will spread that information around in some way. They may spread the information around by talking about the articles with their friends, family or coworkers. Information can travel really quickly when it is released into the world.

Any time a mouse a clicked and every time a keystroke is made, the transmission and retrieval of the information occurs. For most people, the majority of information they process is of the visual kind. Most people do more reading than talking. Hearing and the rest of the senses come after seeing when it comes to the senses which are the ones which provide us with the most information about our surroundings.

We currently live in an information era, and in order to get ahead in today's world, it is necessary to know how to use one's mind effectively to keep a clear head. The information is absolutely abundant today and it is easy for a mind to get overwhelmed by all the information we are presented with daily. There a limit to how much information can be processed by the brain. We live in an age of information overload and we simply haven't evolved to deal with it all.

People simply had to find a way to keep the never-ending flow of data under control. That is why we have systems such as libraries and filing cabinets which keep things organized. That is also why we have machines that take care of crunching numbers such as calculators and computers. In order to achieve some form of organizations, whole new specializations were brought to fruition such as librarians and data analysts.

Even though we have managed to organize it to an impressive level, the capacity of an individual to deal with large amounts of information has remained mostly the same as it always was. Only mother nature can determine how fast the biology will move. This has left the scientific community with no choice but to help people to increase their retention and comprehension of the information. This is also a reason for speed reading being researched by more and more researchers.

Someone who is speed reading does so by skimming through the pages of the text while also attempting to maintain a decent comprehension rate. When people read at their normal default pace of 240 words per minute, their comprehension rate is around three quarters. When speed reading is thrown into the mix, the comprehension rate usually drops to 50%.

There are a plethora of techniques which can be utilized to read faster. Before trying to learn to speed read, it is necessary to learn to breathe properly from the diaphragm and this will ground the reader and place that reader into a headspace which will ensure that the comprehension remains good so that the material can be taken in.

One more technique which can be utilized is the so-called "Wood Method" and this method boils down to using readers hands as a guiding tool so that the attention would remain focused while reading. The hand should be moving without stopping and doing something as simple as this can increase the speed from the average of 240 words per minute to 1000 words per minute.

What keeps the speed reading advocates up at night is the automatic tendency of humans to vocalize what they read. There is an internal speech while the reading takes places which can also be spoken aloud during reading. When this is done, it is made easier for the brain to comprehend what is being read so that the meaning could be extracted from a subject. People do this naturally with the goal of learning and understanding concepts and any attempt to reduce this will make learning that much harder.

It is impossible to get rid of this kind of vocalization in entirety. Since people make an automatic association between how the words look and how they sound. This is very helpful since it makes retrieval of information that much quicker. Words are also a lot easier to remember this way. Vocalization reduces the speed of reading when anything that has to do with the mouth, the jaw or the throat is involved.

There are other things that have to be taken into consideration as well such as someone's level of education, language proficiency, eye health and general mental wellbeing. If any of these things are somewhat impaired, that will really have an effect on how well a person can understand text regardless of the reading speed.

Chapter 13: How to Read Faster

Your goal with speed reading is to read as fast as you can think. Speed is crucial in the age of the information we currently live in. Things happen quickly. Every time you blink an eye, funds are transferred across the globe. Phone and video calls are made as well over the equal distance with similar regularity.

Even people are expected to move as quickly today. The pace of life in big cities is rapid and most people aren't exactly fond of that, even though they are aware that they have to figure out how to handle it all.

Let's imagine, for the sake of the example, a person that works for one of the largest IT companies in a large city as a project manager who manages projects between his end and some country that is halfway across the world. The main means of communications are the phone and an email, along with the occasional travel to a particular country in order to have some face to face interactions with certain people.

During all of this, the employer has to be kept informed about how everything is going so that could get his feedback based on which you could make decisions and keep things under control. Needless to say, there are a lot of things that have to be managed properly and there is a lot of responsibility.

Time is precious and finite and it is necessary to know how to save it so that it doesn't go to waste. One way to do this is to get to the point during the conversations instead of beating around the issue. Similar can be done with email by preferring for the main points of the message to be presented in the form of bullets.

There is also a fair amount of reading which has to be done, whether that means reading through documentation or conducting research by reading books. It is then quite clear why it is necessary to know how to read faster and how to increase the reading speed. When you know how to read faster, you can save so much time. There are things you can do to get your reading speed to a high level.

When you are reading, you don't want to fixate on anything. If your eyes stay on a certain word or a part for too long, then you are doing it wrong. What you need to do is to focus on chunks of words. If you are fluent in a certain language, then the groups of words will make sense to you.

Do what you can to remain mindful. You need to focus if you want to read fast while still comprehending a fair amount of it all. Make sure that distractions and anything that could interrupt you is kept to a minimum so that you could remain mindful. You also want to feel comfortable and well fed since it will be hard to read well if you are thinking about your next meal. The lack of focus can lead to rereading which additionally slows down the whole reading process.

You don't want to get too comfortable, however. If you want to really focus, you should take your reading session seriously. You won't do nearly as well as you could if you do your reading on your bed. You need to be in an environment which will make it easier for you to concentrate. A quiet space that is safe from distractions will do the trick. A library or some similar area where you won't be interrupted is what you should be aiming for.

You also want to make sure that you aren't going back to read the text since the text that is written well usually provides a summary of some kind before moving to the next matter. This is why going back to read really isn't necessary.

Use the cards to help yourself. You can have a card which will always be above the line you are currently on and this will make it harder to go back to the text and to make the mistake of rereading. Maybe you have the confidence because of which you don't constantly have to go back to reread things, but you can still benefit from this card trick. This trick pushes you forward so that you don't slack while reading.

In order to read faster, you should always be working on improving your vocabulary. Any time you come across a word that is unfamiliar, you want to learn about that word so that you understand it. Next time you are faced with that world, your reading process will not come to a halt because of that word.

Teach yourself not to move your lips during your reading. It will take time to get used to this since vocalization is natural to people. The brain is trying to make things easier for itself by attempting to create associations between how the world looks and how it sounds. The habit of vocalizing will slow down your reading every time. Whenever you catch yourself moving your lips, all you have to do is to start reading faster and to focus on groups of words instead of the individual words.

Instead of reading words, you should be reading phrases and sentences. Your eyes span is longer than you think and you actually can read up to 10 words at one time. If you just focus on reading every sixth word, then you will be able to move along so much faster and you probably won't have to worry about vocalizing. When you first try this, you should try it with relatively simple reading material.

Don't just stick to one topic. You want to get used to other topics that are out there. It is natural for people to try to inject some freshness in their lives. If you are reading nonfiction, then you can take a break on the weekends by reading some fiction.

Any time you read something, you want to be aware of the reason for reading that particular material. When you are aware of what you should focus on, you will be able to skim through the pages much quicker since you will be able to quickly tell what is relevant and what is not. It will save you a lot of time if you establish what you want to learn first.

You don't actually have to read each part of the text. It's a myth that you have to read each and every letter in order to understand a book. You should know what you are trying to find out and you can skip some parts if you deem them as unimportant. Reading selectively in this way will make it easier for you to recognize what is essential.

It is a good idea to preview what you will be reading since this will provide you with more context and you will be more prepared. This is similar to seeing the movie trailer before seeing the movie itself. When you take the time to preview the text before reading it, you will be absorbing the information and understanding it so much quicker. In order to preview the text properly, you should preview it from the start to its conclusion while paying attention to headings, subheadings, and bullets. Previewing introduction and conclusion will give you a general understanding of the material.

You should go in with the plan. You will be able to take in the reading material so much more effectively if you are strategic with your approach. You want to know what you want to find out and which questions you want to have answered when reading something. You should have an idea if you can get the answers to those questions based on the goals of the author of the material you are reading.

You want to pace yourself. You will inevitably get a bit tired at some point. When that happens, you can split your reading time into chunks which are between 5 to 10 minutes with periods of rest between them. You want to vary the duration of the reading chunks based on how you are feeling at the moment.

At the end of the day, it all comes back to practice. If you reach the point at which you are finding it difficult to focus on text, you can use your finger as a guiding tool in order to refocus yourself. If you want to increase your focus even further, then you should start moving the finger along even faster. You can increase your reading speed up to 1000 words per minute by doing this.

If you want to read faster, you can use a timer in order to know with certainty how many words you are reading per minute. By timing yourself, you can see if you are improving or not. As your reading speed goes up, make sure that you check if your comprehension can keep up with the increase in speed.

Chapter 14: How Can You Improve Your Comprehension

Comprehension is your ability to understand what something means. Reading is actually among the most complex things that people do. In order to read, you have to recognize a set of symbols through which you should recognize a pattern according to which you would extract the meaning based on what you already know in your mind.

The symbol has to be understood before the meaning behind that symbol could be understood. Anyone who can do such a complex activity well can be considered to be a smart individual.

Comprehension and understanding are vital for someone's mental and social wellbeing. Good comprehension can multiply the success of a person in many areas of life. If a person is able to understand more things while investing less time, then that person will quickly get ahead in life.

Even if comprehension can be increased just slightly, that will go a long way towards making a positive difference in someone's life. That slight increase will compound given enough time and a small difference initially will propel the individual way ahead of the curve.

Small increases over the long period of time tend to multiply and produce larger and larger results over time which can be hard to control in the end. This can work both ways, both for good habits and the bad ones. No one succeeds overnight, but no one fails overnight either. This is why the rich get richer and the poor get poorer.

People who really want to understand a certain topic do so by seeking out books from an author who is an expert on the topic. By reading books, you are saving time and energy by already learning from the experiences of someone else. Learn from the person who has the experience directly is obviously the best course of action, but not everyone can manage that due to a variety of reasons such as finances and time. That's where the reading comes in.

When you are speed reading, you are able to learn more in less time. You have to keep in mind that your comprehension rate gets lowered to 50% even though you could be reading 1000 words per minute. The average person can read around 240 words per minute while comprehending around three quarters of what he reads. If this rate of comprehension could be improved, then a lot of doors could start to open for that person.

Learning how to speed read is actually easier than learning how to comprehend even more. If someone wants to improve their comprehension, that person has to be willing to grow. There are ways to improve comprehension and that is the focus of this chapter.

In order to increase your comprehension, you should start working on your self-assessment skills. If you want to see how good your comprehension is, you can test that by creating a summary of the material you finished reading. You know that you understand something when you can explain it in your own words. The more you do this, the better at it you will be.

You want to try to push the limits of your comprehension. You can test your comprehension by filling out questionnaires and doing crossword puzzles. All of this can be done by yourself from the comfort of your own home.

If you want for your comprehension to improve, your metacognition has to improve. Metacognition is the capacity to think about thoughts. This is very useful for noticing unproductive thoughts in someone's head. This enables a person to analyze their thoughts to see if those thoughts make sense. This is what eastern philosophy is about. It is about being able to be honest with yourself.

You should always keep an open mind to comprehend more and to be more receptive to new ideas. You should have a reading habit. If you come from a learning background, you have better chances of being able to comprehend more. The more subjects and more fields someone reads about, the higher the chance that the person will be able to comprehend more by making connections in their mind.

Communication skills also have to be up to par. Talking with people of different socioeconomic backgrounds goes a long way since everyone has an opinion about something. You may not always agree with different opinions, but there is always a possibility of learning something new.

Even though reading a lot is certainly a good thing, you have to take the time to contemplate and to think about what you have read since that is how you give time to the ideas to really sink into your mind. It is recommended to play around with an idea a little before automatically accepting it as it is and that is what critical thinking is all about.

Conclusion

Speed reading can offer quite a few benefits in today's world, especially for people such as students and business people. It makes all the sense in the world to learn how to speed read with all the information we are bombarded with day after day. Anyone would love to be able to deal with their inbox much faster.

Speed reading enhances your learning ability which can open all kinds of doors and opportunities for you. Speed reading teaches you how to focus on one challenging thing at a time, which less and less people can do these days. You will also be able to relax more since focusing allows you to enter into the flow state which is very calming and meditative.

You are also bound to discover some new interests and to rekindle old ones. You can also become more creative and a better problem because of speed reading since you will be able to make connections faster.

Knowledge is power and the ones who can draw from many ideas and combine them have better odds of getting ahead and getting what they want. More knowledge can benefit you in many ways and it can allow you to speak more confidently since you have more to draw from, both in personal and professional life. Don't forget to apply the knowledge since that is how wisdom is formed. Wisdom is the ability to see 100 pathways and to know with certainty which one is the right one.

I hope that you have enjoyed this book and that you have found it useful. If you want to share your thoughts about this book, then you can do so by leaving a review on the Amazon page. Have a great rest of the day!

Printed in Great Britain
by Amazon